Meditation for New Moms

*A Postpartum Essential
for the Self-Care of
New Moms*

Shannon Lesley

TABLE OF CONTENTS

INTRODUCTION

    Motherhood did not come to me lightly. My mother passed away on a Monday. The following Friday, just four days later, my daughter was born. I was in labor at a hospital 2,000 miles away during my mother's funeral. I hadn't even had time to grieve my mother before postpartum depression struck. I wasn't producing enough milk, so my baby was nursing nonstop. No one tells you about the chapped nipples or that your nipples might bleed—you just find out one day, pained and humiliated. On top of the pain from nursing, I had injuries from a traumatic birth that made it painful to sit until I finally got corrective surgery three months later. While I was considered a "new mom" because I had never given birth before, I actually had two other children—one son through adoption and one stepson. This new baby was demanding all the attention I was used to giving my boys. This baby was breaking my connection to the children I had built my life around, and I resented her for it.

On top of all that, my daughter was colicky. She cried constantly. She cried when she was hungry, she cried in the car, she cried when she woke up, she cried when the sun touched her, she cried when anyone picked her up or put her down... she cried, she cried, she cried. She almost never slept because sleep would have interrupted her crying! I thought babies were supposed to sleep a lot.

What was wrong with mine? I remember adding up the minutes of sleep I got the night before, and if I pieced together less than four hours of sleep, I knew it was going to be a rough day.

I felt so worn down and tired. I cried too—all the time. Until one day I stopped, and that was worse. In fact, it was downright scary.

When I stopped crying, I felt like there was nothing left of me. I was just a hollow shell going through the motions. I considered suicide, but honestly, the entire act sounded like more energy than I could muster. I considered giving away my baby, which seemed like a pretty good idea at the time. I even had a few different plans for how to give her away. Fortunately, the antidepressants my obstetrician gave me started to help just in time for me to stop considering that fantasy.

I kept going to baby groups and therapy

sessions, but I wasn't really there. It was just a fog of me. Nothing helped or changed anything until one day my therapist got an idea.

She asked, "If I record a meditation for you, would you listen to it while you nurse?"

"Sure, whatever," I said. I had never meditated before.

She pulled out one of those old-fashioned cassette recorders that journalists used to use in the 60s, with a small plastic microphone, and started talking into it softly. I watched her and wondered where I was going to find a cassette player. I guess I found one, though I don't remember doing so. What I do remember is every word of that meditation. I listened to it over and over and over. I listened to it so many times that even when I wasn't home, I could close my eyes and hear that voice in my head and find the calm the meditation offered.

That meditation, made just for me, is what saved my life and my family. Everything I went through that year, and the meditation that saved me, has inspired me to write this book for you, from one mom to another. My goal is to pay it forward and help new moms relax so they can find the joy and confidence associated with motherhood.

Motherhood is one of the hardest things you can do in life. The reassurance of being seen is often nice. I am unbelievably grateful to every single mother who saw me struggling during my journey and reached out to help. We women are so powerful. The way we stick together and help each other out is really special. This book is my way of seeing you. Each chapter is its own meditation created specially to help you out. Find the one that speaks to you most, and listen to it while nursing, falling asleep, while your baby sleeps, or whenever you need it.

I want you to know that I see you and I'm

so proud that you are pushing forward. Taking care of yourself is taking care of your baby too. You are not alone. I am here with you, and I care about you immensely. My hope is that this book allows you to come to terms with motherhood and how it impacts you, providing you with healthy coping mechanisms and support along the way.

And, in case you are wondering what happened to that baby I almost gave away: She's a teenager now. It turned out that I had given birth to my best friend that year. I'm eternally appreciative for the support that allowed me to keep my baby daughter, and every mother should feel supported in that way too.

Without further ado, let's proceed to the first meditation.

TIME FOR A VACATION

The first meditation tool I will guide you through is a guided imagery meditation that is intended to provide you with a vacation from everything. You will be able to travel away from your worries, stressors, and anything else you simply need a break from, and just take a few moments to truly relax. Before you begin any meditation, it is important to come to a relaxed state. For this specific meditation, I want you to find a quiet, comfortable place.

Using ear plugs or borrowing your baby's white noise machine can help you along if you do not have a place inside of your home that seems peaceful enough.

Once you have placed yourself into a comfortable position in an ideal space, rest your eyes. Let them come to a close or hold a soft gaze if that's more comfortable for you, releasing any tension in your face at the same time. Inhale deeply, noticing how your body holds the breath. Feel it in your chest and stomach, the air traveling down within your body. Exhale gently, allowing your chest to fall back down as you do so. We're going to take a few deeper, calming breaths just like this, noticing how the air travels through the body and how it feels in the nose. Allow your mind to rest. If a thought arises, notice it and let it go. Don't force those thoughts out or berate yourself; just acknowledge them and let them move on. Continue focusing on your breath in the meantime. Feel your worries begin to distance themselves for now; focus on the present. Anything else can wait for now.

I want you to imagine yourself standing beside a vibrantly green forest in the prime of its life. A small path waits just ahead to guide you through. Step toward the path, listening to the gentle ripple of the breeze in the leaves of the forest. Now enter the forest, remaining on the path. Breathe in and out. Feel the crisp air of nature enter your lungs as you breathe along with the trees. Notice the different types of trees and how the shapes and textures of the trunks and leaves vary. Allow yourself to walk along this path for a few moments, noticing everything from the grass to the sky while you breathe the fresh air in and out, in and out.

The trail comes to a bend, and you notice an animal sleeping on a large, flat stone nestled gently between some trees. You slowly walk toward the animal, taking note of what kind it is. As you approach, they wake up and notice you. As they do, feel your body flood with a sense of calm and protection. You were meant to stumble across them today on your journey. Your new companion stretches before leaping to the ground and walking along the very same path you arrived on. They check to ensure you are ready to follow, and then you two set off along the path together.

The path up ahead forks, and your animal companion guides you to the left. Continue along the trail, breathing in and out. Notice what you hear. The birds, playful and awake in the trees, chirp to each other. Let the sound fill your ears and pay attention to how carefree they are as you walk. You're enjoying the day along with them. Remember to keep walking at your own pace, taking in as much of nature as you would like to—there's nothing in the world to rush for. Right now, this walk is just for you.

You notice the path under you begins to transform into one that is more wooden, oak planks interlacing each other gently, and a handrail rests beside you. As you step onto it, your ears pick up the soft sounds of a flowing stream underfoot. You're on a low, beautiful bridge that is carrying you across some water, clear blue and serene. Watch the leaves and flowers and sticks and bubbles float along the river for a moment, noticing the breeze playing with your hair and the water meeting the rocks below. Spend a few moments with the river—your animal friend awaits–and continue walking when you are ready.

Just as the path returns to normal, a bend presents itself in front of you. The trees are starting to be just a tad bit scarcer, and you notice beautiful wildflowers beginning to join the grass alongside the trail. Purples, pinks, blues, and whites pattern the plush green grass as you walk through the bend. Take a look above you; the trees have made a beautiful tunnel-like space inside this corner. Vines hug the tree branches, creating a break in the sunlight peeking through above and instead replacing it with a canopy.

On the other end of the bend, the path ends, and you come to the entrance of a large, open, grassy field. The grass is lighter here, and the warm sunlight kisses the whole area, trees remaining faithfully to the sides of the field. The wildflowers you noticed moments ago are now abundant, coating the field in color. You see bees bustling around in the area, and they leave you be as you work, and you smile at them as you venture farther into the field. Your animal companion stretches again and then curls up in the grass, ready for another easy nap as you explore once again.

Breathe in and notice the flowery and light scent of your surroundings grace your senses. Breathe out. Allow your knees to bend and sink into the tall, soft grass just next to your animal. Lay back with them, allowing your body to rest on the safety of the grass around you. Spread your fingers out, brushing through the grass and the wildflowers alike.

How do the petals feel in between your fingers? What about the leaves? And the grass? Carefully caress the grass as you lay there, gazing gently at the sky above. Blue and cloudless, and more beautiful than you have ever seen it before, watch how the sky changes as the afternoon sun turns into evening dusk. Breathe in and out—let yourself rest. Notice your eyes come to a soft, restful close as you lay in the grass.

With your eyes closed, slowly allow yourself to return to your body in the present. Breathe in and out a few more times, once again noticing how the air swells within your body. Open your eyes gently, giving yourself time to adjust to the lights and environment you are in. Don't rush the return to the present—this process is essential in allowing the restful state to last. Slowly, begin to wiggle your fingers and toes, letting the life return to your body. Stretch your arms up and out, feeling the muscles in your arms and back as you do. Sit up when you are ready if you did

13

the meditation lying down. Continue breathing for a few cycles.

After a meditation, especially one of this nature, I like to continue about my day by first setting an intention or speaking a few affirmations. That way, my mind and body know what to expect and feel even on a subconscious level. Intentions or affirmations can be just one word or a full sentence. One of my favorites is, "I am worthy of peace and love," and you can align yours with either something you need or something you hope to achieve. If this seems too much right now, pick a word you want to represent your day. Think about it to yourself, and then thank your mind and body for being here with you now. It's important to be thankful to your mind for guiding and supporting you and your body.

As you finish out this meditation, you should feel far more relaxed and rested from your nature vacation. Remember that you can return to this meditation anytime you need a break, and you can change anything you need to suit yourself. Feel free to use the same concept to explore other locations, environments, and areas of nature, being mindful of your surroundings as you do so.

Now that you have finished this guided imagery meditation, you can continue on with your day! If that stress begins to return, your animal companion and nature will be there to soothe you once again.

HARNESSING THE STRENGTH OF YOUR MATERNAL ANCESTORS

During the first year of motherhood, a recurring thought I kept close was especially helpful in keeping me going and providing me with both pride and strength. This meditation is based on that thought and is a visualization meditation. You can do this meditation alone or with your baby present, holding them in your arms as you meditate. The purpose of this meditation is to connect to the strength of your maternal ancestors and the babies they raised successfully, so if having your baby present helps, I encourage you to include them if you can. If not, this meditation will work just as effectively with your baby elsewhere for the time being. Do what suits you best.

Sit in a comfortable spot, such as a rocking chair or glider. You might plant your feet firmly on the ground beneath you or kick them up and recline. As you work with this meditation, your baby might be asleep near you, playing near you, or something else if you have opted to include them—do not necessarily worry about keeping them silent. Allow your eyes to come to a close or maintain a soft gaze, either on an unspecified object in the room or on your baby.

We're going to start by calming the breath. Breathe in and out slowly, not forcing your breath into a rhythm but instead allowing it to come to a natural, calm rate. This meditation is best intended for when you need strength and encouragement to continue being the best mother possible for your baby. Because of this, you may have a number of worries, doubts, or concerns clouding your mind. I want you to imagine them like clouds and that your mind is a bright, blue sky, obscured by those thoughts. One of the most important lessons I've learned is to not condemn negative or upsetting thoughts and to, instead, allow them to just exist. So, I want you to notice those clouds. Pay attention to their shape and color, and watch as they float away, leaving the sky of your mind blank and blue once again. As you continue steadying your breath, repeat that imagery as much as you need to; let a thought roll in as a cloud, then roll away, leaving you in peace. Keep the sky in your mind.

Once you feel your breath has reached a restful pace and your mind is sufficiently clear, you can begin the meditation. To begin, I want you to think about all the mothers in your family who came before you. Prior to your birth, your mother had a mother, and her mother had a mother, all the way back to the dawn of humanity. Over and over again, the women in your family and in your history gave birth to children who gave birth to children of their own. These people—the women and babies dating all the way back to the beginning of your family line—all have something in common with you. They were all mothers.

Inhale and exhale, keeping your breath steady. Every single one of them, these women in your family line who came before you, survived. They had a baby and kept it alive, as you are doing now. That baby grew into a wonderful adult who had a baby and succeeded as well. Not one person in your entire lineage failed at this task; otherwise, we would not be here today. This, understandably, required so much strength and courage on the part of each mother.

Today, you are going to connect to their bravery and strength—this is the strength of your maternal ancestors. You are going to gain the ability to recognize yourself as a part of that strong line of women who succeeded in raising their babies.

Remember the sky that represents your thoughts? Good, because we aren't finished with it. I want you to imagine a red string connecting the heart of your baby to the heart of yourself. Imagine that string connecting you to the sky, traveling up into the atmosphere and into the Heavens, universe, or space. Visualize it connecting you to all of the mothers in your lineage who came before you, heart to heart, all the way back through history. This string connects all of you through your strength, femininity, and the true power of motherhood.

Make sure your breath remains steady. Spend a few beats focusing on this breath, feeling and visualizing the connection of the string between you and every woman before you in your lineage. Now, visualize the very first woman in your family. Think of what she might look like, be that in spirit form or during her time on Earth. Imagine this powerful woman and the line connecting her to you through all of your ancestors, starting with the very first mother of your family lineage. Visualize the very first woman sending you energy through that line from her heart, passing through every other woman along the way. You can visualize this as a white light, or any other colored light, coating the red string. As it passes through each woman, see it get brighter and stronger as it builds with the strength and courage each mother has ever experienced.

Inhale and hold your breath for a moment as you imagine that energy—the strength, power, and bravery—coming down to you through the string. Exhale as it enters your heart, letting it warm you. This effectively allows you to harness the strength of your maternal ancestors. Accept the love and encouragement your ancestors are offering. They are your personal groupies; your fan club; your cheerleaders, wanting to see you succeed and find joy. Inhale and exhale for a few beats.

Then, visualize the strings disappearing, connecting just you and your baby. You can either imagine the strings dissolving and being absorbed into each mother's heart or simply disconnecting from one another temporarily. Through the red string binding you and your baby, send your baby love and compassion. One day, they and their children, and all of the mothers after you, will be able to appreciate the strength you had as well.

As you close off the meditation, visualize the strength you have been sent in your heart, and feel it spread through your body, from your head to your toes. Let it travel through your belly—the same incredible place that carried your baby—and think about how amazing you and your body are. Every day, you wake up to take care of a beautiful little life, and that's something to be proud of. Thank yourself for being so courageous and allow the strength of your maternal ancestors to linger in your body. Imagine the string between you and your baby disappearing as well, with the energy you sent them lingering in their little body for safekeeping.

Take a few more deep, soothing breaths, and then open your eyes slowly. Allow yourself to come back to the present moment, both mind and body. Remember that your ancestors are one support network that will never leave you in the shadows; you can always return to them through this meditation and harness some more strength if you feel it slipping. There is an infinite amount of energy and strength that can be passed on to you; it goes back generations. Whenever you need it, remember to clear your mind's sky and allow that red string to connect each and every woman back to yourself.

Finally, as we end this meditation, allow yourself to feel pride. Allow yourself to think about how awesome and amazing you are. You're a mother, and that's one of the strongest things anyone can do. It's also important to be proud of where you come from. You are one in a long, long line of survivors who came before you. You rock! You can now continue about your day feeling strong and proud of your status as a mother, with the sound knowledge that you can handle anything that comes at you.

NURSING MOMS

Think about it for a second: Your body is able to provide your baby with all of the nutrients they need during the first part of their life. Isn't that amazing? Your body comes programmed with the impressive ability to not just provide life, but to sustain it as well. Lactation and breastfeeding can often be painful and anxiety inducing. Through this meditation, which combines aspects of focused attention and body scan meditations, you will begin to feel more comfortable with your body that has changed to nurse your baby. You will appreciate your body and recognize your ability to nurse for what it is— one of the most amazing feats possible.

You can do this meditation before, during, or after nursing your baby. Either way, you will be focusing on your breath, mind, and body, so feel free to use this to prepare to nurse, soothe the mind while nursing, or relax after nursing. The first step to this meditation is to find a relaxing space to practice, one that is relatively quiet and calm. If you are doing this while nursing your baby, get into a comfortable position so you will not have to move much or be disturbed for the next few minutes. Otherwise, you can get comfortable in any way you would like. The best position to be in for this meditation is one where your spine is long and your low back is relaxed; however, do not sacrifice comfort for posture.

We're going to start with the focused

attention portion of this meditation. This will allow you to relax completely. I want you to start by inhaling for five seconds, slowly. Allow the breath to enter your lungs, expanding the chest, and then hold it for five seconds. You may now exhale. Allow your breath to fall into a slow but natural rhythm now without forcing anything. Focus your attention on your chest right now and how the breath expands and contracts in your lungs, in and out, up and down. If your baby is resting on your chest, notice how they smell. Feel the gentle pressure of them as you breathe in and out.

Continue breathing like this for a few minutes, about five of them. I want you to think while you do. Think about your role as a mother who nurses. Within your body are all of the nutrients your baby needs to live and grow into a healthy toddler. You hold so much power by taking on this role. Think about how amazing that is, sustaining the life of your little baby. You are truly amazing.

Continue to breathe and feel the rise and fall of your chest. Think about the changes your body has experienced throughout pregnancy and during nursing. Your body has become a soft, comfortable, safe place for your baby to rest close to you. Imagine how loved they must feel, warm in your arms. Every single change your body has experienced, good or bad, has allowed your baby to be here and be healthy. You are allowing your baby to share in your body for now, and that is so selfless and wonderful of you. Every time you nurse your baby, you can think about how you are the single most important person in their world, nurturing them softly and protecting them.

Keep breathing slowly and calmly. We are now going to scan the body. If possible, let the bottoms of your feet rest on the ground. Notice how your feet feel, just your feet. How does the fabric or object touching them feel? What temperature are they? Give your toes a wiggle and feel where the tension in your feet exists. Every day, your feet carry you and your baby like they did during your pregnancy. How incredible!

Allow your focus to travel up your legs, noticing how they feel and if anything is sore, tense, hot or cold. You can imagine this like a copy machine, scanning with light from one end of your body to the next. Move up to the knees, thighs, and waist, slowly and calmly focusing on each area. All of these body parts let you care for your baby. Each and every part of your body is vital and important, especially as you nurse and continue to care for your baby. Pay attention to how your lower body feels as you nurse, prepare to nurse, or rest from just having nursed. Breathe in and out again, and let's move on within our meditation.

The scan continues; pay attention to how your belly feels and then your back and shoulders, focusing on all these parts individually as you move up the body. Allow any tension to release, letting your shoulders sink and back relax. Notice anywhere you feel a particular sensation as you go. Allow your belly to expand freely with your breath, and let your spine naturally curve and relax. Don't worry about your posture right now; focus on releasing the tension within this part of your body. Then, continue on.

Pay special attention to your chest when you get there. Notice any pain, soreness, or anything particularly striking about how you feel right there. This is the focus point of our meditation because it is where your baby eats. Remember that even if you feel pain or frustration, nursing in spite of the pain allows your baby to survive. The pain will not last forever, but the nutrients your baby receives will provide them about 80 years of life in all. That is so wonderful and strong. *You* are so wonderful and strong. Think about the sensation of your baby resting on your chest and remember how phenomenal your body is in these moments.

If it helps, you can visualize what is happening during lactation scientifically, picturing the nutrients flowing from you to your baby. Inside of your breasts, there are cell clusters that are somewhat like grapes. Dozens of these exist within your breasts, and they are responsible for producing milk. That milk flows through tunnel-like passageways in the breasts, allowing the breast milk to flow out. This is how your milk gets to the baby. Once you come to this part in the meditation, take a few moments to visualize how this operation flows, nurturing your baby in the most natural way possible. Your body knows exactly what to do, all on its own. After becoming familiar with this process and the visualization involved, continue the body scan.

Allow your attention to travel down your arms, wiggling your fingertips as you do. Continue breathing deeply. Your arms carry your baby every single day—lifting, changing, loving them. Your arms allow you to hold them close to your chest as you nurse, filling their tiny body with everything it needs and supporting them all the while. Breathe in and out. Even on days it seems hard, remember that your arms are probably your baby's favorite place, especially when you embrace them into your warm chest. Allow your focus to travel up your face, relaxing any tension within the muscles. Focus on your beautiful face, the same one that smiles and laughs with your baby. Focus on softening any tension in your eyes especially, remembering that your baby takes such solace in the gentle gazes you give them, learning so much about life and about you through such simple means as eye contact.

Every single part of you from your head to your feet is magical. You singlehandedly have the capacity to create and nourish life. In just the simple act of allowing your baby to nurse, you are doing one of the most incredible things any human could ever do, and you should be proud of yourself for it.

As we close out this meditation, I want you to snuggle your baby close as you continue to breathe, feeling their warmth and the tiny, yet otherworldly, pressure of them on your chest. Your baby is grateful for everything you do for them. Touch your baby softly, breathing in and out, and remember that no matter what, they count on you, and that is such a beautiful thing. Even when it is stressful, even when it is challenging, there is so much beauty in the feminine ability to nurse your little baby.

Continue breathing in and out for a few beats. If you enjoy soothing breathing exercises or struggle to regulate your breath, I encourage you to do something called square breathing. During this practice, you inhale, hold, and exhale your breath for the same amount of seconds. It's a lovely way to encourage deep, mindful breaths, and will help you calm down during the process of nursing. Beginning or ending meditations with square breathing is beneficial, and even if you do not have time to meditate, coaching yourself through the process of square breathing will slow the mind and ease your stress. Feel free to close off this meditation with some square breathing.

To do so, select a number from one to ten. This is how many seconds each section of the square breathing will take. Most people find six or eight seconds to be ideal. Begin by breathing in for that number of seconds. As you do so, envision your breath crawling up the left side of a square, slowly reaching the top as you finish your inhale. Hold your breath for the same amount of time, allowing time to inch along the upper side of the square. Exhale as your breath climbs down the right side of the square. Once you've fully exhaled, you can optionally wait for the same amount of seconds to inhale again, completing the bottom side of the square. You may repeat the process as necessary until you feel calmer.

Slowly open your eyes if you've closed them and allow the life to come back to your body, focusing on the here and now. Whenever you find yourself struggling with nursing, preparing to nurse, or calming down after nursing, just remember how amazing it is that your body can do that. No one else can do that for your baby, only you. Nursing creates a special bond unlike any other. You are stellar for doing what you do and persevering. Make sure to give yourself the credit you deserve for caring for your baby, and with time and strength, it will all be alright. Keep your head up, Mama.

MOMMY NEEDS A NAP

Finding time to rest and relax as a mother can be incredibly challenging. Often, as soon as you find yourself sleeping deeply, the baby will begin to cry. Or maybe your baby has finally settled down, but you can't seem to calm your mind enough to allow yourself to sleep. I understand this feeling; it has happened to me more times than I can count. This meditation will guide you into a relaxed state, allowing you to sleep, even if it is just a five-minute nap. You deserve rest.

This meditation can be returned to any time you need. A combination of guided imagery, breath work, and progressive muscle relaxation will allow your body to naturally slow and find the calm it needs to sleep. The results of this meditation will come to you best if you allow yourself to awaken naturally; however, if you absolutely need to wake up by a specific time, set an alarm with a gentle tone to lull you out of sleep. A restful waking process helps a peaceful sleep benefit you throughout the day. Once you have sorted out your location and needs, we can proceed.

The first thing I want you to do is lay down somewhere. Once your baby is safe, you can lay with them in your bed alone or wherever is most comfortable for you. You can even rest on the couch or another surface, whatever you have will work. Make sure you have a pillow and blankets and that the room is a good temperature in which you feel comfortable resting. I want you to lay down in whatever position is most comfortable to you. I recommend laying on your back for the sake of this meditation, but you can truly do it in any position you think will be most conducive to your sleep.

Furthermore, you can still do this meditation if your baby needs to nurse. My favorite position that I used while nursing and sleeping with my baby was to lie on my side, so the mattress could support both the baby and me. This allowed me to rest while feeding my baby and was truly a life-changing technique! Once you've laid down with the lights off, no distracting noises around, and your phone silenced and put away, we can begin the meditation.

Make sure your pillows are in the right spot and your blanket is covering you. Place your hands somewhere comfortable. Maybe that's on your belly, under the pillow, or somewhere else. Find a good spot for them to rest. We're going to start by clearing your mind. As a mother, one of the hardest parts about getting to sleep can be worrying about your baby or other responsibilities that you have. You can't sleep with these things burdening your mind, though. So what we need to do is give these thoughts a bit of space and then free our minds from them. Before you sleep right now, you are going to have one opportunity to think about anything that's worrying you, no matter how specific or random.

When the first thought enters your mind, acknowledge it. Allow yourself to think, "Okay, here is this thought. I have acknowledged it, and now I'm moving on for the moment. I deserve relaxation and peace tonight and every other night, and I will not allow this thought to disturb that." In this way, you are simultaneously noticing the thought and affirming to yourself that it is alright to move on from your troubles and worries. Repeat the process of noticing and sending off your thoughts without judgment until you find your mind at peace from these thoughts. Don't spend the whole night dwelling; at some point, it is okay to stop acknowledging thoughts, and think to yourself, "I have acknowledged that I worry and am doubtful about things. I am not going to let this interrupt my rest tonight." After doing so, maintain a clear mind by focusing on your breath.

In order to let yourself rest, you need to allow your body to relax. Lying still, start with your focus at the top of your head. We are going to work on relaxing any tension in your entire body, a little at a time. Untense your forehead, and allow your eyelids to droop softly, keeping them closed after doing so. Unclench your jaw, allowing a natural separation to form between the top and bottom rows of your teeth. Let your tongue remain light in your mouth. Doesn't that feel better already?

You've undoubtedly had a difficult day, week, month, or even year. Right now, there is nothing you need to do besides rest. Self-care is a priority—you cannot care for others while neglecting yourself. You cannot give yourself the life you deserve if you place anything and everything above you. Release the tension in your shoulders, allowing them to remain delicately untensed, and work your way down the spine. Let go of any tension in the belly and back as you continue, letting your mattress, or whatever bedding you might have, absorb your weight. For now, allow the bed and I to take care of you. Don't worry about anything. If thoughts begin to reenter your mind, simply remind them that they can return tomorrow. Now is you-time, and you are just going to sleep.

Continue to breathe softly, listening to the way the air enters and exits through your nose or mouth. Pay special attention to your stomach, how the breath swells and releases within you. Listen to your heartbeat, the steady rhythm of life within you. Listening to your own breathing or heartbeats are both wonderful ways to soothe yourself into sleep. Then allow your hips to rest; unclench your joints or muscles, and just let your hips rest against the bed. They are so tired from carrying you, just like you are tired. Let them rest.

Feel the tension dissolve from the tops of your thighs and knees. With every breath, feel your body loosening more and more, being supported by the concaves of your bed. All there is to do right now is sleep, resting your mind, body, and spirit. Allow your calves to relax, your ankles to rest, and release any remaining tension in your feet. If you notice that you've tensed up a part of your body as we've continued through this meditation, drop the tension now without judgment. Notice it and let it go.

Keep listening to the sound of yourself breathing in and out. Imagine that your breath is like the waves of an ocean, ebbing and flowing. Inhale as the tide recedes, giving way to damp sand and inching closer toward the sun setting at the horizon. Exhale as the tide expands back toward the shore. Let the gentle whooshing sounds fill your ears as you breathe in and out. The sun is setting over your horizon and being replaced by the loving, radiant moon as the sky darkens. All the animals in the ocean are beginning to rest as the tide calms. It's time for the world to go to sleep for a little while, letting everything from the day before remain in the past, and letting everything to come stay in the future. Right now, just sleep. Sleep.

I want to leave you with a few words of compassion and validation as you sleep. Don't force yourself to stay awake to listen to me, just rest. You are doing an amazing job. Every single day, you wake up and you care for someone besides yourself, and that's not something everyone can say they do. It's truly a brave and wonderful job you have.

Everything you worry about, no matter how silly it may seem, no matter how upsetting it might feel, is normal. Other mothers like you experience the same worries; you are not alone. You are one of thousands of amazing women doing the best they can. Don't let those negative thoughts negate what you are doing. Raising a child, especially your first one, is a lot of trial and error. I promise you are doing an amazing job.

I want you to have the very sweetest of dreams; I hope you wake up feeling rested and safe, knowing that you can come back to practice any time you need to find peace and relaxation before bed. You are seen and appreciated. Just like you take care of your baby, allow this to be my way of caring for you—gently tucking you in for a good night's rest. Everything is going to be alright. Just sleep.

Good night, Mama.

WORKING MOMS

This is a meditation for working moms, no matter what that job may be. If you are looking at this and feel it is not the meditation for you, I invite you to stay with an open mind. A working mom is a working mom. If you work in an office, a diner, or somewhere else, you are a working mom. If you take care of your baby full time, staying at home to clean and feed and otherwise care for the baby, you too are a working mom. Your job is your job regardless of if it provides you with financial benefit. If it contributes to the betterment and well-being of your baby's life, then I consider it a job and you should too. Providing is providing.

For mothers working away from home, it can be really hard to be separate from their babies. The younger they are, the harder that separation can seem. You just gave life to this little being, and now you have to spend so much time away from them. You may feel like all you want to do is make sure they're safe and within your eyesight. It can make you feel anxious or even guilty for being so far away from your baby. Even if you work from home, feeding and caring for your baby, the full-time job of doing so can wear on you. I also want to take the time to acknowledge that even if you feel relief at having time away from your baby, you are valid. That guilt can still exist because it feels like you should crave being with your baby when, in reality, work seems like the better place to be. No matter if you prefer to be at work or home, you are valid in how you feel, and I see you. Every single aspect of being a working mother can be challenging. Regardless of what you are doing, it can feel overwhelming and scary—how do you know you are doing the right thing for your baby?

This meditation combines loving kindness and noting techniques to help you cope with working constantly, no matter if you are with or away from your beloved baby. You can listen to and follow this meditation while you are working, regardless of where your job takes place. You do not have to be alone or even comfortable for this; we're just going to focus on the mind and the breath. All you need is a few moments where you can work without thinking about the task or even take a bit of a break. Just a few moments of your thoughts are all I need today.

Start by noting any particularly obvious tensions in your body and release them. Try to find a position where your posture can relax but where your mind is alert. Sitting in an office chair or otherwise upright is perfect for this. Allow your hands to fall to your lap or your wrists to remain relaxed if you must use your hands. Relax your eyes as well, optionally closing them if you are able to do so. We are going to first engage in a noting practice. Start by being aware of your body and how it feels, paying attention to sensations and feelings.

Go from the top to the bottom of your body, releasing tension and noting how you feel. First, start with the head, focusing on any sensations, tightness, emotions, etc., that arise. Let your attention travel down the face, loosening the jaw and resting the tongue, and proceed to your shoulders. Untense those shoulders, letting them drop to a natural resting position. Again, continue to notice any sensations that arise as you do so. Travel down the spine, elongating it but holding no tension there, and then focus on the legs and feet. Take note of how every part of your body feels throughout this process. At the end of this scan, rest on the sensation of your breathing.

As your mind and body come to a state of peace, you will notice thoughts come to the forefront of your mind. Just note that they exist. Don't worry about labeling them, judging them, or feeling any certain way about them. Just let them be. Pay attention to how they make you feel, but do not worry about the label or anything like that. As you let them go, imagine a strong, sturdy box. Place your thoughts into the box and set the box aside. We aren't condemning them; rather, they are being saved later, when you can access them at a more appropriate time.

Now, I want you to set an intention for this meditation. Something you could set, for instance, is, "I know that being a working mother is good for me and my baby." Anything you want to set for your intention works. Once you've done that, I want you to think about your baby. Truly bring to mind their image. Think about what they look like, how you dress them, the way they smell, and the color of their eyes. Imagine your baby in your mind much like they were with you. Now, think about the feelings that you have for your baby. Allow those feelings to come to your mind as you think about your child. Love, compassion, and joy might be emotions you feel, but it is possible that sadness, guilt, or anxiety come to mind as well. Whatever feelings you feel about your baby are valid; they do not indicate what kind of parent you are at all. Even if your baby makes you sad, it is not your fault nor your baby's. Those are normal feelings.

The purpose of thinking about your baby during this meditation is to remind yourself that you are doing this for them. I want you to take a few deep breaths in through your nose, pausing, and then exhaling through your mouth. You're doing good—just a few more breaths just like that.

Mama, your baby is safe right now, wherever they are. The work you are doing is good for them, even if you are not with them right now. Providing for your baby financially is honorable; it gives them life and the resources they need to survive. Working in the home is also an honorable choice. Whichever you have chosen is the right choice for you, your baby, and the family you are building.

Continue to breathe in and out, keeping the image of your baby in your mind. Think about what else they will gain from you working. If you have a baby daughter, she will grow to admire you as a role model. She will know that women are strong and can do anything because her mom managed to both raise her successfully and work at the same time. If you have a baby son, he will learn to respect the power women have and value women, understanding that we are just as strong as men. Your baby will, no matter what, understand that you are strong, and they can be the same way too. They will know that providing for their kids one day is a powerful and brave choice.

Imagine your baby in a safe environment, no matter where that may be to you. Maybe it is in a crib, on the floor, or in the arms of a loving relative or caregiver. You may even choose to picture your baby in your own arms. Visualize them being safe and feeling loved. As we close out this meditation, I want you to think or speak the following affirmations to yourself: "I am strong and doing what is best for my baby. Working is good for my baby, and I am making the right choices right now." Repeat this phrase as many times as you need, breathing deeply all the while.

When you are finished meditating, simply open your eyes and return to your job. You've got this, and I believe in you! You're doing great.

IT'S OKAY EVEN WHEN IT'S NOT OKAY: FINDING ACCEPTANCE WHEN THINGS AREN'T GOING THE WAY YOU PLANNED

Raising a child, notoriously, does not come with a manual. As mothers, we go through so many struggles on a daily basis that it feels exhausting. While little hurdles can be dealt with, there are some bigger ones that you might be struggling with that you do not know how to handle. From a colicky baby to an unhelpful co-parent and from a lack of emotional attachment to struggles with nursing, things outside of our control as mothers can hurt. That goes especially for things we "should" be able to do. This meditation is for any mother struggling with raising their baby because it is not going as anticipated. Breathwork, visualization, and skillful compassion meditation techniques will teach you how to accept a situation and find peace within it.

Chances are, you feel overwhelmed or even panicked. To start, find a place where you can be alone or alone with your baby if you are their sole caregiver. I recommend finding a dark and quiet room or somewhere with less stimuli than your living room. We're going to start with some deep, calming breaths. Before we can rationally think about what is going on, we need to find a few moments of calm.

Close your eyes. Inhale slowly through your nose as deeply as you can. Exhale through the mouth and pay attention to your body as you do. If you are feeling anxious right now, there may be some tightness in the chest or stomach, shaky feelings in the limbs, or other physical manifestations of anxiety. As you inhale, allow the air to fill your lungs and work to push that tightness away.

Let me talk to you for a moment as you breathe. Right now, everything might seem way too hard for you to handle. I need you to know that just because it is hard doesn't mean you've done anything wrong. Motherhood is meant to be difficult, or else we wouldn't make such a big deal out of giving birth. But it is a very, very challenging experience. It's important to understand that it will not always be this hard, even if it feels like it will be. As humans and mothers, it is okay and even expected to be imperfect. These struggles teach you things that you will need for future chapters of your child's life. Each and every lesson will make every day after today easier. For now, just accept that you are doing the best you can with what you can control. Don't be mad at yourself—anything you are experiencing right now is a natural part of the process. Hiccups along the road are not your fault.

Listen to and think about what I've said as you continue to breathe. It's essential that you know this is all part of the process. This breathing pattern is especially helpful for panic attacks, anger, frustration, or intense crying; take as long as you need to just breathe and be. Continue to breathe in and out. Imagine your lungs like bright, red balloons, filling with air as you inhale, expanding. Let the air leave, being replaced by calm and comfort instead. Continue to fill and empty your lungs with this imagery in mind. Just focus on the in and out, in and out.

Once you feel like you can breathe a bit better, it is time to learn how to perform a skillful compassion meditation. Skillful compassion allows you to practice effective self-compassion, which is very important for motherhood. Self-compassion is going to be what you need to make it through hard moments like this. The first thing that I need you to do is think about what caused you to become so stressed out today. I know that, in reality, the combination of things piling up has caused this, but just focus on one thing at a time. What was the straw that broke the camel's back for you today? Hold that event or situation in your mind, and truly think about it. Notice the way it makes you feel. Do you feel it in a part of your body? Does it cause physical discomfort to think about?

As this sits with you, repeat the following affirmation to yourself: "I am struggling right now." You might think that that's a rather obvious "affirmation," but by clearly thinking or speaking that out loud, you are validating how you feel in the moment about the situation effectively. This makes sure that you aren't just noticing the emotions, but that you are noticing what caused them as well. Continue to breathe deeply in and out, through the nose and mouth, while you validate how you feel. You are experiencing something difficult.

Continue to allow your breath to soothe you, flowing in and out of your lungs. Focus on the rise and fall of your chest. The next part of practicing skillful compassion is to validate that your experience is normal. Keep your issue in mind, the struggles and negative feelings associated with it existing, judgment-free. Now, I want you to affirm to yourself: "Struggling is a natural part of life." It's important to understand this; everyone struggles, especially new mothers. Reassure yourself that it's okay and normal to struggle. I struggled, your mother struggled, and her mother did too. Take a deep breath in and let it out again. These struggles don't last forever, and it's not a bad thing that they exist in the first place. Think of how much you're learning about life and your baby. In the end, these struggles will make you much stronger and much wiser.

The final step in practicing skillful compassion is to pull in the compassion. Affirm to yourself: "I will grant myself acceptance and peace. It is okay for me to struggle. I am allowed to struggle." It won't always be this hard, mom. An important part of being able to accept yourself and your circumstances is to allow yourself to be forgiving and gracious. This includes being forgiving of yourself and your capacity for feeling stressed or upset. It can be especially challenging to allow yourself space for forgiveness and acceptance, even when you are forgiving of others. Think of one of your best friends and imagine her in your shoes. How would you comfort her? If she felt like everything was going wrong, what would you say to her? Now, practice saying those same things to yourself, with compassion and kindness. Allow yourself to feel like it will be okay.

I want to guide you through one final visualization to finish off this meditation. We're going to focus on imagery and your breath. Inhale and exhale slowly and deeply. Square breath if it's helpful, inhaling for eight seconds, holding the breath, and then exhaling for eight seconds. Repeat this a few times over until you have fallen into the steady in and out rhythm of this breathing pattern.

I want you to imagine your heart in your chest. Imagine it clearly, either shaped like an anatomical or geometrical heart , the choice is yours. Imagine it is being filled with a radiating gold light. Let your heart shine. Now, I want your next few breaths to be incredibly mindful so we can focus on your struggles and accept them. Exhale as deeply as you can. As you do so, imagine all of your struggles, worries, and issues being expelled from your body, out of your nose or mouth. Then, imagine yourself inhaling them once again, but instead of simply letting them re-enter your body, let them go to your heart. Breathe them into your heart, filled with golden, healing light, and let your heart give them a warm hug. Imagine the beautiful, sun-like light surrounding the issues that you're facing and replace the dread with compassion and self-empathy. If you need to, continue breathing out struggle and pain and then breathing it in once again, letting your heart neutralize the pain with self-love and compassion.

Continue to breathe with me for just a few moments before we finish this meditation. In and out, slow and steady. I care about you, and it's important to me that you know that everything is going to be alright. Even if things aren't going how you planned, each and every struggle you face will allow you to come out stronger in the end. Your baby has such a strong, wonderful mother to look up to, and you should be proud of yourself. Take as long as you need to breathe and find calm within yourself before returning to the present. Don't worry, you've got this!

WHEN CRISIS STRIKES

Because motherhood is extremely challenging, it can be tough to know who you should reach out to when you need more help than you alone can provide for yourself and your baby. Be it mental, physical, or financial aid you are looking for, it is vital to know where to turn to for assistance. This chapter is a quick list of resources that can be beneficial to mothers.

If you are in need, do not hesitate to reach out to any of the following resources; they exist with the explicit purpose of helping people like you. If you need assistance, some resources worth looking into include:

- Crisis nurseries: The purpose of a crisis nursery is to provide emergency childcare for families in crisis, including overnight care. To locate your nearest crisis nursery, simply look up "crisis nursery near me" and go from there.

- Postpartum support: For those struggling with postpartum depression, resources are available. Visit www.postpartum.net for various resources and tools, including a hotline that can be called or texted as well as support groups and educational tools.

- Suicide prevention resources: Postpartum depression can take a major toll on a mother's life, even if depression has never been an issue before. If you find yourself struggling with thoughts of harming yourself, visit 988lifeline.org. This website contains information on one of the major suicide and crisis lines that you can call if you need help. If you would like a number to call directly, dial 1-800-273-TALK to speak to a crisis professional. Calling hotlines like these does save lives, and I highly recommend doing so if you need someone to speak to. Another option for suicide prevention is to visit your nearest emergency room (with your baby if you do not have a second parent or family member in your life to care for them in your absence). From there, the ER will assist you in getting the care you need.

- Resources for other mental illnesses: Visit www.nami.org. There, you will find both educational tools and resources for mental health issues.

- Domestic violence resources: Visit www.thehotline.org. Not only does this site offer resources and aid for those suffering from domestic abuse, but it offers a call and chat line as well. The site also includes tips for quickly and safely backing out of the site for those in dangerous situations. If you or your baby are suffering from domestic violence or threats surrounding domestic violence, please reach out.

- The Special Supplemental Nutrition Program for Women, Infants, and Children (WIC): If you need resources or aid in providing food for yourself and your family, visit www.fns.usda.gov/wic to apply for WIC.

- Low-income support: Having a baby is very expensive, which is why programs like Welcome Baby exist. On welcomebabyusa.org, you can learn how to receive a care package of items your infant needs catered specifically to low-income families.

I know reaching out for help can be a very scary experience or even guilt-inducing. I also know that reaching out for help is one of the bravest and strongest things a woman can do. If you need help from any of the sources above, I encourage you to make contact as soon as possible. The people involved with running these resources are judgment-free and safe and have the interest of you and your baby in mind. Please do not hesitate to get the things you need.

CONCLUSION

I hope you found one or a few of these meditations to be beneficial in relieving your stress and validating your experiences with motherhood. No matter what, it is important to know that things will be okay. Whether you are a mother who works, stays at home, raises multiple kids, is experiencing the struggles of parenting alone, or experiences anything in between, by taking care of yourself, you are also taking care of your baby. They need you to be healthy and strong and the best version of yourself that you can be. Remember that you are not alone and that your struggles are very common for mothers of new babies.

The fact you have finished this book means you want what is best for you and your baby, and I could not be prouder of you. I want to thank you from the bottom of my heart for allowing me to take you on this journey and provide you with these tips. I know they saved me when I needed support as a new mom, and I hope they have been able to do the same for you.

If you found these meditations to be beneficial, please consider leaving the book a review. That's the best way to allow other new mothers to see and benefit from these resources, and it is an easy way for you to support other mothers as well. If more mothers have access to these resources, we can all contribute to destigmatizing and demystifying the stress and struggles associated with motherhood.

Thank you again for spending this valuable time with me and hearing what I have to offer you as a new mother. Even when things are at their hardest, remember that you can revisit these resources and meditations whenever you need them. They will be here for you.

You've got this, Mom!

ABOUT THE AUTHOR

Shannon Lesley is a mom of three kids, three different ways: one step kid, one foster adopted kid and one birth kid. In comparison to her two older kids, birthing her third child was the worst—she does not recommend it. Lesley is experienced in extreme post-partum depression and the kind of anxiety that makes her get up in the middle of the night to make sure her kids are still breathing. She is passionate about children and education, and proud of her work as an ambassador for foster youth, a girl scout leader and a teacher. *Meditation for New Moms* is Lesley's first book.

www.ingramcontent.com/pod-product-compliance
Lightning Source LLC
Chambersburg PA
CBHW051235120626
46547CB00013B/1654